M000308773

To

_____

From

_____

Date

_____

The joy of the Lord is your strength.
Nehemiah 8:10

Christian art gifts®

© Christian Art Gifts, RSA
Christian Art Gifts Inc., IL, USA
Printed in China

The path of the just is as the shining light,
that shineth more and more unto the perfect day.

~ *Proverbs 4:18*

Arise, shine; for thy light is come, and
the glory of the LORD is risen upon thee.

~ Isaiah 60:1

The name of the LORD is a strong tower:
the righteous runneth into it, and is safe.

~ Proverbs 18:10

"Blessed are the pure in heart: for they shall see God."

~ Matthew 5:8

For the eyes of the Lord are over the righteous,
and His ears are open unto their prayers.

~ 1 Peter 3:12

Blessed is every one that feareth the LORD; that walketh in His ways. For thou shalt eat the labour of thine hands: happy shalt thou be, and it shall be well with thee.

~ *Psalm 128:1-2*

The LORD is good to all: and His tender mercies are over all His works.

~ *Psalm 145:9*

Being confident of this very thing, that He which hath begun a good work in you will perform it until the day of Jesus Christ.

~ *Philippians 1:6*

And of His fulness have all we received, and grace for grace.

~ John 1:16

Oh that men would praise the LORD for His goodness, and for His wonderful works to the children of men! For He satisfieth the longing soul, and filleth the hungry soul with goodness.

~ Psalm 107:8-9

And we know that all things work together for good to them that love God, to them who are the called according to His purpose.

~ Romans 8:28

For the LORD God is a sun and shield: the LORD
will give grace and glory: no good thing
will He withhold from them that walk uprightly.

~ Psalm 84:11

For the LORD is good; His mercy is everlasting;
and His truth endureth to all generations.

~ *Psalm 100:5*

The LORD taketh pleasure in them that
fear Him, in those that hope in His mercy.

~ Psalm 147:11

"If thou canst believe, all things are possible to him that believeth."

~ Mark 9:23

Eye hath not seen, nor ear heard, neither have
entered into the heart of man, the things
which God hath prepared for them that love Him.

~ 1 Corinthians 2:9

Behold, the eye of the LORD is upon them that fear Him, upon them that hope in His mercy.

~ *Psalm 33:18*

But my God shall supply all your need
according to His riches in glory by Christ Jesus.

~ Philippians 4:19

There are many devices in a man's heart;
nevertheless the counsel of the LORD, that shall stand.

~ Proverbs 19:21

And therefore will the LORD wait, that He may be gracious unto you, and therefore will He be exalted, that He may have mercy upon you.

~ Isaiah 30:18

The LORD hath prepared His throne in the heavens;
and His kingdom ruleth over all.

~ Psalm 103:19

Blessed be the God and Father of our Lord Jesus Christ, who hath blessed us with all spiritual blessings in heavenly places in Christ.

~ *Ephesians 1:3*

Thou wilt shew me the path of life: in Thy presence is fulness of joy; at Thy right hand there are pleasures for evermore.

~ Psalm 16:11

Mercy unto you, and peace, and love, be multiplied.

~ Jude 2

The blessing of the LORD, it maketh rich,
and He addeth no sorrow with it.

~ Proverbs 10:22

Now the God of hope fill you with all joy and peace in believing, that ye may abound in hope, through the power of the Holy Ghost.

~ Romans 15:13

God be merciful unto us, and bless us;
and cause His face to shine upon us.

~ Psalm 67:1

Cause me to hear Thy lovingkindness in the morning;
for in Thee do I trust: cause me to know the way
wherein I should walk; for I lift up my soul unto Thee.

~ Psalm 143:8

Cast thy burden upon the LORD, and He shall sustain thee: He shall never suffer the righteous to be moved.

~ *Psalm 55:22*

The LORD shall preserve thee from all evil: He shall preserve thy soul. The LORD shall preserve thy going out and thy coming in from this time forth, and even for evermore.

~ Psalm 121:7-8

Trust in the LORD with all thine heart; and lean not unto thine own understanding. In all thy ways acknowledge Him, and He shall direct thy paths.

~ Proverbs 3:5-6

Rejoice evermore. Pray without ceasing.
In every thing give thanks: for this is the
will of God in Christ Jesus concerning you.

~ 1 Thessalonians 5:16-18

The path of the just is as the shining light,
that shineth more and more unto the perfect day.

~ Proverbs 4:18

Arise, shine; for thy light is come, and
the glory of the LORD is risen upon thee.

~ Isaiah 60:1

The name of the LORD is a strong tower:
the righteous runneth into it, and is safe.

~ *Proverbs 18:10*

"Blessed are the pure in heart: for they shall see God."

~ Matthew 5:8

For the eyes of the Lord are over the righteous,
and His ears are open unto their prayers.

~ 1 Peter 3:12

Blessed is every one that feareth the LORD; that walketh in His ways. For thou shalt eat the labour of thine hands: happy shalt thou be, and it shall be well with thee.

~ *Psalm 128:1-2*

The LORD is good to all: and His tender mercies are over all His works.

~ Psalm 145:9

Being confident of this very thing, that He which hath begun a good work in you will perform it until the day of Jesus Christ.

~ *Philippians 1:6*

And of His fulness have all we received, and grace for grace.

~ John 1:16

Oh that men would praise the LORD for His goodness, and for His wonderful works to the children of men! For He satisfieth the longing soul, and filleth the hungry soul with goodness.

~ Psalm 107:8-9

And we know that all things work together for good to them that love God, to them who are the called according to His purpose.

~ Romans 8:28

For the LORD God is a sun and shield: the LORD
will give grace and glory: no good thing
will He withhold from them that walk uprightly.

~ Psalm 84:11

For the LORD is good; His mercy is everlasting;
and His truth endureth to all generations.

~ Psalm 100:5

The LORD taketh pleasure in them that
fear Him, in those that hope in His mercy.

~ Psalm 147:11

"If thou canst believe, all things are possible to him that believeth."

~ Mark 9:23

Eye hath not seen, nor ear heard, neither have
entered into the heart of man, the things
which God hath prepared for them that love Him.

~ 1 Corinthians 2:9

Behold, the eye of the LORD is upon them that fear Him, upon them that hope in His mercy.

~ Psalm 33:18

But my God shall supply all your need
according to His riches in glory by Christ Jesus.

~ Philippians 4:19

There are many devices in a man's heart;
nevertheless the counsel of the LORD, that shall stand.

~ *Proverbs 19:21*

And therefore will the LORD wait, that He may be gracious unto you, and therefore will He be exalted, that He may have mercy upon you.

~ Isaiah 30:18

The LORD hath prepared His throne in the heavens;
and His kingdom ruleth over all.

~ Psalm 103:19

Blessed be the God and Father of our Lord Jesus Christ, who hath blessed us with all spiritual blessings in heavenly places in Christ.

~ *Ephesians 1:3*

Thou wilt shew me the path of life: in Thy presence is fulness of joy; at Thy right hand there are pleasures for evermore.

~ *Psalm 16:11*

Mercy unto you, and peace, and love, be multiplied.

~ *Jude 2*

The blessing of the LORD, it maketh rich,
and He addeth no sorrow with it.

~ *Proverbs 10:22*

Now the God of hope fill you with all joy and peace in believing, that ye may abound in hope, through the power of the Holy Ghost.

~ *Romans 15:13*

God be merciful unto us, and bless us;
and cause His face to shine upon us.

~ Psalm 67:1

Cause me to hear Thy lovingkindness in the morning;
for in Thee do I trust: cause me to know the way
wherein I should walk; for I lift up my soul unto Thee.

~ *Psalm 143:8*

Cast thy burden upon the LORD, and He shall sustain thee: He shall never suffer the righteous to be moved.

~ *Psalm 55:22*

The LORD shall preserve thee from all evil: He shall preserve thy soul. The LORD shall preserve thy going out and thy coming in from this time forth, and even for evermore.

~ Psalm 121:7-8

Trust in the LORD with all thine heart; and lean not unto thine own understanding. In all thy ways acknowledge Him, and He shall direct thy paths.

~ Proverbs 3:5-6

Rejoice evermore. Pray without ceasing.
In every thing give thanks: for this is the
will of God in Christ Jesus concerning you.

~ 1 Thessalonians 5:16-18

The path of the just is as the shining light,
that shineth more and more unto the perfect day.

~ Proverbs 4:18

Arise, shine; for thy light is come, and
the glory of the LORD is risen upon thee.

~ Isaiah 60:1

The name of the LORD is a strong tower:
the righteous runneth into it, and is safe.

~ *Proverbs 18:10*

"Blessed are the pure in heart: for they shall see God."

~ Matthew 5:8

For the eyes of the Lord are over the righteous,
and His ears are open unto their prayers.

~ 1 Peter 3:12

Blessed is every one that feareth the LORD; that walketh in His ways. For thou shalt eat the labour of thine hands: happy shalt thou be, and it shall be well with thee.

~ *Psalm 128:1-2*

The LORD is good to all: and His tender mercies are over all His works.

~ *Psalm 145:9*

Being confident of this very thing, that He which hath begun a good work in you will perform it until the day of Jesus Christ.

~ *Philippians 1:6*

And of His fulness have all we received, and grace for grace.

~ John 1:16

Oh that men would praise the LORD for His goodness, and for His wonderful works to the children of men! For He satisfieth the longing soul, and filleth the hungry soul with goodness.

~ Psalm 107:8-9

And we know that all things work together for good to them that love God, to them who are the called according to His purpose.

~ Romans 8:28

For the LORD God is a sun and shield: the LORD
will give grace and glory: no good thing
will He withhold from them that walk uprightly.

~ Psalm 84:11

For the LORD is good; His mercy is everlasting;
and His truth endureth to all generations.

~ *Psalm 100:5*

The LORD taketh pleasure in them that
fear Him, in those that hope in His mercy.

~ *Psalm 147:11*

"If thou canst believe, all things are possible to him that believeth."

~ Mark 9:23

Eye hath not seen, nor ear heard, neither have
entered into the heart of man, the things
which God hath prepared for them that love Him.

~ 1 Corinthians 2:9

Behold, the eye of the LORD is upon them that fear Him, upon them that hope in His mercy.

~ *Psalm 33:18*

But my God shall supply all your need
according to His riches in glory by Christ Jesus.

~ Philippians 4:19

There are many devices in a man's heart;
nevertheless the counsel of the LORD, that shall stand.

~ *Proverbs 19:21*

And therefore will the LORD wait, that He may be gracious unto you, and therefore will He be exalted, that He may have mercy upon you.

~ Isaiah 30:18

The LORD hath prepared His throne in the heavens;
and His kingdom ruleth over all.

~ *Psalm 103:19*

Blessed be the God and Father of our Lord Jesus Christ, who hath blessed us with all spiritual blessings in heavenly places in Christ.

~ *Ephesians 1:3*

Thou wilt shew me the path of life: in Thy presence is fulness of joy; at Thy right hand there are pleasures for evermore.

~ Psalm 16:11

Mercy unto you, and peace, and love, be multiplied.

~ *Jude 2*

The blessing of the LORD, it maketh rich,
and He addeth no sorrow with it.

~ *Proverbs 10:22*

Now the God of hope fill you with all joy and peace in believing, that ye may abound in hope, through the power of the Holy Ghost.

~ *Romans 15:13*

God be merciful unto us, and bless us;
and cause His face to shine upon us.

~ Psalm 67:1

Cause me to hear Thy lovingkindness in the morning;
for in Thee do I trust: cause me to know the way
wherein I should walk; for I lift up my soul unto Thee.

~ Psalm 143:8

Cast thy burden upon the LORD, and He shall sustain thee: He shall never suffer the righteous to be moved.

~ *Psalm 55:22*

The LORD shall preserve thee from all evil: He shall preserve thy soul. The LORD shall preserve thy going out and thy coming in from this time forth, and even for evermore.

~ Psalm 121:7-8

Trust in the LORD with all thine heart; and lean not unto thine own understanding. In all thy ways acknowledge Him, and He shall direct thy paths.

~ Proverbs 3:5-6

Rejoice evermore. Pray without ceasing.
In every thing give thanks: for this is the
will of God in Christ Jesus concerning you.

~ 1 Thessalonians 5:16-18

The path of the just is as the shining light,
that shineth more and more unto the perfect day.

~ Proverbs 4:18

Arise, shine; for thy light is come, and
the glory of the LORD is risen upon thee.

~ Isaiah 60:1

The name of the LORD is a strong tower:
the righteous runneth into it, and is safe.

~ *Proverbs 18:10*

"Blessed are the pure in heart: for they shall see God."

~ Matthew 5:8

For the eyes of the Lord are over the righteous,
and His ears are open unto their prayers.

~ 1 Peter 3:12

Blessed is every one that feareth the LORD; that walketh in His ways. For thou shalt eat the labour of thine hands: happy shalt thou be, and it shall be well with thee.

~ *Psalm 128:1-2*

The LORD is good to all: and His tender mercies are over all His works.

~ *Psalm 145:9*

Being confident of this very thing, that He which hath begun a good work in you will perform it until the day of Jesus Christ.

~ *Philippians 1:6*

And of His fulness have all we received, and grace for grace.

~ John 1:16

Oh that men would praise the LORD for His goodness, and for His wonderful works to the children of men! For He satisfieth the longing soul, and filleth the hungry soul with goodness.

~ *Psalm 107:8-9*

And we know that all things work together for good to them that love God, to them who are the called according to His purpose.

~ Romans 8:28

For the LORD God is a sun and shield: the LORD
will give grace and glory: no good thing
will He withhold from them that walk uprightly.

~ Psalm 84:11

For the LORD is good; His mercy is everlasting;
and His truth endureth to all generations.

~ *Psalm 100:5*

The LORD taketh pleasure in them that
fear Him, in those that hope in His mercy.

~ *Psalm 147:11*

"If thou canst believe, all things are possible to him that believeth."

~ Mark 9:23

Eye hath not seen, nor ear heard, neither have
entered into the heart of man, the things
which God hath prepared for them that love Him.

~ 1 Corinthians 2:9

Behold, the eye of the LORD is upon them that fear Him, upon them that hope in His mercy.

~ Psalm 33:18

But my God shall supply all your need
according to His riches in glory by Christ Jesus.

~ Philippians 4:19

There are many devices in a man's heart;
nevertheless the counsel of the LORD, that shall stand.

~ Proverbs 19:21

And therefore will the LORD wait, that He may be gracious unto you, and therefore will He be exalted, that He may have mercy upon you.

~ Isaiah 30:18

The LORD hath prepared His throne in the heavens;
and His kingdom ruleth over all.

~ Psalm 103:19

Blessed be the God and Father of our Lord Jesus Christ, who hath blessed us with all spiritual blessings in heavenly places in Christ.

~ *Ephesians 1:3*

Thou wilt shew me the path of life: in Thy presence is fulness of joy; at Thy right hand there are pleasures for evermore.

~ Psalm 16:11

Mercy unto you, and peace, and love, be multiplied.

~ *Jude 2*

The blessing of the LORD, it maketh rich,
and He addeth no sorrow with it.

~ *Proverbs 10:22*

Now the God of hope fill you with all joy and peace in believing, that ye may abound in hope, through the power of the Holy Ghost.

~ *Romans 15:13*

God be merciful unto us, and bless us;
and cause His face to shine upon us.

~ *Psalm 67:1*

Cause me to hear Thy lovingkindness in the morning;
for in Thee do I trust: cause me to know the way
wherein I should walk; for I lift up my soul unto Thee.

~ Psalm 143:8

Cast thy burden upon the LORD, and He shall sustain thee: He shall never suffer the righteous to be moved.

~ *Psalm 55:22*

The LORD shall preserve thee from all evil: He shall preserve thy soul. The LORD shall preserve thy going out and thy coming in from this time forth, and even for evermore.

~ Psalm 121:7-8

Trust in the LORD with all thine heart; and lean not unto thine own understanding. In all thy ways acknowledge Him, and He shall direct thy paths.

~ Proverbs 3:5-6

Rejoice evermore. Pray without ceasing.
In every thing give thanks: for this is the
will of God in Christ Jesus concerning you.

~ 1 Thessalonians 5:16-18

The path of the just is as the shining light,
that shineth more and more unto the perfect day.

~ Proverbs 4:18

Arise, shine; for thy light is come, and
the glory of the LORD is risen upon thee.

~ Isaiah 60:1

The name of the LORD is a strong tower:
the righteous runneth into it, and is safe.

~ Proverbs 18:10

"Blessed are the pure in heart: for they shall see God."

~ Matthew 5:8

For the eyes of the Lord are over the righteous,
and His ears are open unto their prayers.

~ 1 Peter 3:12

Blessed is every one that feareth the LORD; that walketh in His ways. For thou shalt eat the labour of thine hands: happy shalt thou be, and it shall be well with thee.

~ *Psalm 128:1-2*

The LORD is good to all: and His tender mercies are over all His works.

~ *Psalm 145:9*

Being confident of this very thing, that He which hath begun a good work in you will perform it until the day of Jesus Christ.

~ Philippians 1:6

And of His fulness have all we received, and grace for grace.

~ John 1:16

Oh that men would praise the LORD for His goodness, and for His wonderful works to the children of men! For He satisfieth the longing soul, and filleth the hungry soul with goodness.

~ Psalm 107:8-9

And we know that all things work together for good to them that love God, to them who are the called according to His purpose.

~ Romans 8:28

For the LORD God is a sun and shield: the LORD
will give grace and glory: no good thing
will He withhold from them that walk uprightly.

~ *Psalm 84:11*

For the LORD is good; His mercy is everlasting;
and His truth endureth to all generations.

~ *Psalm 100:5*

The LORD taketh pleasure in them that fear Him, in those that hope in His mercy.

~ *Psalm 147:11*

"If thou canst believe, all things are possible to him that believeth."

~ Mark 9:23

Eye hath not seen, nor ear heard, neither have
entered into the heart of man, the things
which God hath prepared for them that love Him.

~ 1 Corinthians 2:9

Behold, the eye of the LORD is upon them that fear Him, upon them that hope in His mercy.

~ *Psalm 33:18*

But my God shall supply all your need
according to His riches in glory by Christ Jesus.

~ Philippians 4:19

There are many devices in a man's heart;
nevertheless the counsel of the LORD, that shall stand.

~ Proverbs 19:21

And therefore will the LORD wait, that He may be gracious unto you, and therefore will He be exalted, that He may have mercy upon you.

~ Isaiah 30:18

The LORD hath prepared His throne in the heavens;
and His kingdom ruleth over all.

~ Psalm 103:19

Blessed be the God and Father of our Lord Jesus Christ, who hath blessed us with all spiritual blessings in heavenly places in Christ.

~ *Ephesians 1:3*

Thou wilt shew me the path of life: in Thy presence is fulness of joy; at Thy right hand there are pleasures for evermore.

~ *Psalm 16:11*

Mercy unto you, and peace, and love, be multiplied.

~ *Jude 2*

The blessing of the LORD, it maketh rich,
and He addeth no sorrow with it.

~ Proverbs 10:22

Now the God of hope fill you with all joy and peace in believing, that ye may abound in hope, through the power of the Holy Ghost.

~ *Romans 15:13*

God be merciful unto us, and bless us;
and cause His face to shine upon us.

~ *Psalm 67:1*

Cause me to hear Thy lovingkindness in the morning;
for in Thee do I trust: cause me to know the way
wherein I should walk; for I lift up my soul unto Thee.

~ Psalm 143:8

Cast thy burden upon the LORD, and He shall sustain thee: He shall never suffer the righteous to be moved.

~ *Psalm 55:22*

The LORD shall preserve thee from all evil: He shall preserve thy soul. The LORD shall preserve thy going out and thy coming in from this time forth, and even for evermore.

~ Psalm 121:7-8

Trust in the LORD with all thine heart; and lean not unto thine own understanding. In all thy ways acknowledge Him, and He shall direct thy paths.

~ Proverbs 3:5-6

Rejoice evermore. Pray without ceasing.
In every thing give thanks: for this is the
will of God in Christ Jesus concerning you.

~ 1 Thessalonians 5:16-18

The path of the just is as the shining light,
that shineth more and more unto the perfect day.

~ Proverbs 4:18

Arise, shine; for thy light is come, and
the glory of the LORD is risen upon thee.

~ Isaiah 60:1

The name of the LORD is a strong tower:
the righteous runneth into it, and is safe.

~ Proverbs 18:10

"Blessed are the pure in heart: for they shall see God."

~ Matthew 5:8

For the eyes of the Lord are over the righteous,
and His ears are open unto their prayers.

~ 1 Peter 3:12

Blessed is every one that feareth the LORD; that walketh in His ways. For thou shalt eat the labour of thine hands: happy shalt thou be, and it shall be well with thee.

~ Psalm 128:1-2

The LORD is good to all: and His tender mercies are over all His works.

~ *Psalm 145:9*

Being confident of this very thing, that He which hath begun a good work in you will perform it until the day of Jesus Christ.

~ Philippians 1:6

And of His fulness have all we received, and grace for grace.

~ John 1:16

Oh that men would praise the LORD for His goodness, and for His wonderful works to the children of men! For He satisfieth the longing soul, and filleth the hungry soul with goodness.

~ Psalm 107:8-9

And we know that all things work together for good to them that love God, to them who are the called according to His purpose.

~ Romans 8:28

For the LORD God is a sun and shield: the LORD
will give grace and glory: no good thing
will He withhold from them that walk uprightly.

~ *Psalm 84:11*

For the LORD is good; His mercy is everlasting;
and His truth endureth to all generations.

~ *Psalm 100:5*

The LORD taketh pleasure in them that
fear Him, in those that hope in His mercy.

~ *Psalm 147:11*

"If thou canst believe, all things are possible to him that believeth."

~ Mark 9:23

Eye hath not seen, nor ear heard, neither have
entered into the heart of man, the things
which God hath prepared for them that love Him.

~ 1 Corinthians 2:9

Behold, the eye of the LORD is upon them that fear Him, upon them that hope in His mercy.

~ *Psalm 33:18*

But my God shall supply all your need
according to His riches in glory by Christ Jesus.

~ Philippians 4:19

There are many devices in a man's heart;
nevertheless the counsel of the LORD, that shall stand.

~ Proverbs 19:21

And therefore will the LORD wait, that He may be gracious unto you, and therefore will He be exalted, that He may have mercy upon you.

~ Isaiah 30:18

The LORD hath prepared His throne in the heavens;
and His kingdom ruleth over all.

~ Psalm 103:19

Blessed be the God and Father of our Lord Jesus Christ, who hath blessed us with all spiritual blessings in heavenly places in Christ.

~ Ephesians 1:3

Thou wilt shew me the path of life: in Thy presence is fulness of joy; at Thy right hand there are pleasures for evermore.

~ *Psalm 16:11*

Mercy unto you, and peace, and love, be multiplied.

~ Jude 2

The blessing of the LORD, it maketh rich,
and He addeth no sorrow with it.

~ Proverbs 10:22

Now the God of hope fill you with all joy and peace in believing, that ye may abound in hope, through the power of the Holy Ghost.

~ Romans 15:13

God be merciful unto us, and bless us;
and cause His face to shine upon us.

~ *Psalm 67:1*

Cause me to hear Thy lovingkindness in the morning;
for in Thee do I trust: cause me to know the way
wherein I should walk; for I lift up my soul unto Thee.

~ Psalm 143:8

Cast thy burden upon the LORD, and He shall sustain thee: He shall never suffer the righteous to be moved.

~ *Psalm 55:22*

The LORD shall preserve thee from all evil: He shall preserve thy soul. The LORD shall preserve thy going out and thy coming in from this time forth, and even for evermore.

~ Psalm 121:7-8

Trust in the LORD with all thine heart; and lean not unto thine own understanding. In all thy ways acknowledge Him, and He shall direct thy paths.

~ Proverbs 3:5-6

Rejoice evermore. Pray without ceasing.
In every thing give thanks: for this is the
will of God in Christ Jesus concerning you.

~ 1 Thessalonians 5:16-18

The path of the just is as the shining light,
that shineth more and more unto the perfect day.

~ Proverbs 4:18

Arise, shine; for thy light is come, and
the glory of the LORD is risen upon thee.

~ Isaiah 60:1

The name of the LORD is a strong tower:
the righteous runneth into it, and is safe.

~ Proverbs 18:10

"Blessed are the pure in heart: for they shall see God."

~ *Matthew 5:8*

For the eyes of the Lord are over the righteous,
and His ears are open unto their prayers.

~ 1 Peter 3:12

Blessed is every one that feareth the LORD; that walketh in His ways. For thou shalt eat the labour of thine hands: happy shalt thou be, and it shall be well with thee.

~ *Psalm 128:1-2*

The LORD is good to all: and His tender mercies are over all His works.

~ Psalm 145:9

Being confident of this very thing, that He which hath begun a good work in you will perform it until the day of Jesus Christ.

~ Philippians 1:6

And of His fulness have all we received, and grace for grace.

~ John 1:16

Oh that men would praise the LORD for His goodness, and for His wonderful works to the children of men! For He satisfieth the longing soul, and filleth the hungry soul with goodness.

~ Psalm 107:8-9

And we know that all things work together for good to them that love God, to them who are the called according to His purpose.

~ Romans 8:28

For the LORD God is a sun and shield: the LORD
will give grace and glory: no good thing
will He withhold from them that walk uprightly.

~ Psalm 84:11

For the LORD is good; His mercy is everlasting;
and His truth endureth to all generations.

~ Psalm 100:5

The LORD taketh pleasure in them that
fear Him, in those that hope in His mercy.

~ *Psalm 147:11*

"If thou canst believe, all things are possible to him that believeth."

~ Mark 9:23

Eye hath not seen, nor ear heard, neither have
entered into the heart of man, the things
which God hath prepared for them that love Him.

~ 1 Corinthians 2:9

Behold, the eye of the LORD is upon them that fear Him, upon them that hope in His mercy.

~ *Psalm 33:18*

But my God shall supply all your need
according to His riches in glory by Christ Jesus.

~ Philippians 4:19

There are many devices in a man's heart;
nevertheless the counsel of the LORD, that shall stand.

~ Proverbs 19:21

And therefore will the LORD wait, that He may be gracious unto you, and therefore will He be exalted, that He may have mercy upon you.

~ Isaiah 30:18

The LORD hath prepared His throne in the heavens;
and His kingdom ruleth over all.

~ Psalm 103:19

Blessed be the God and Father of our Lord Jesus Christ, who hath blessed us with all spiritual blessings in heavenly places in Christ.

~ Ephesians 1:3

Thou wilt shew me the path of life: in Thy presence is fulness of joy; at Thy right hand there are pleasures for evermore.

~ Psalm 16:11

Mercy unto you, and peace, and love, be multiplied.

~ *Jude 2*

The blessing of the LORD, it maketh rich,
and He addeth no sorrow with it.

~ Proverbs 10:22

Now the God of hope fill you with all joy and peace in believing, that ye may abound in hope, through the power of the Holy Ghost.

~ Romans 15:13

God be merciful unto us, and bless us;
and cause His face to shine upon us.

~ Psalm 67:1

Cause me to hear Thy lovingkindness in the morning;
for in Thee do I trust: cause me to know the way
wherein I should walk; for I lift up my soul unto Thee.

~ *Psalm 143:8*

Cast thy burden upon the LORD, and He shall sustain thee: He shall never suffer the righteous to be moved.

~ *Psalm 55:22*

The LORD shall preserve thee from all evil: He shall preserve thy soul. The LORD shall preserve thy going out and thy coming in from this time forth, and even for evermore.

~ Psalm 121:7-8

Trust in the LORD with all thine heart; and lean not unto thine own understanding. In all thy ways acknowledge Him, and He shall direct thy paths.

~ Proverbs 3:5-6

Rejoice evermore. Pray without ceasing.
In every thing give thanks: for this is the
will of God in Christ Jesus concerning you.

~ 1 Thessalonians 5:16-18

The path of the just is as the shining light,
that shineth more and more unto the perfect day.

~ Proverbs 4:18

Arise, shine; for thy light is come, and
the glory of the LORD is risen upon thee.

~ Isaiah 60:1

The name of the LORD is a strong tower:
the righteous runneth into it, and is safe.

~ *Proverbs 18:10*

"Blessed are the pure in heart: for they shall see God."

~ Matthew 5:8

For the eyes of the Lord are over the righteous,
and His ears are open unto their prayers.

~ 1 Peter 3:12

Blessed is every one that feareth the LORD; that walketh in His ways. For thou shalt eat the labour of thine hands: happy shalt thou be, and it shall be well with thee.

~ Psalm 128:1-2

The LORD is good to all: and His tender mercies are over all His works.

~ *Psalm 145:9*

Being confident of this very thing, that He which hath begun a good work in you will perform it until the day of Jesus Christ.

~ *Philippians 1:6*

And of His fulness have all we received, and grace for grace.

~ John 1:16

Oh that men would praise the LORD for His goodness, and for His wonderful works to the children of men! For He satisfieth the longing soul, and filleth the hungry soul with goodness.

~ *Psalm 107:8-9*

And we know that all things work together for good to them that love God, to them who are the called according to His purpose.

~ Romans 8:28

For the LORD God is a sun and shield: the LORD
will give grace and glory: no good thing
will He withhold from them that walk uprightly.

~ Psalm 84:11

For the LORD is good; His mercy is everlasting;
and His truth endureth to all generations.

~ Psalm 100:5

The LORD taketh pleasure in them that fear Him, in those that hope in His mercy.

~ *Psalm 147:11*